DEATH UNCOVERED

NEAR-DEATH EXPERIENCES

Meghan Gottschall

full tilt PRESS

Near-Death Experiences
Death Uncovered

Full Tilt Press
42964 Osgood Road
Fremont, CA 94539
readfulltilt.com

Full Tilt Press publications may be purchased for educational, business, or sales promotional use.

Editorial Credits

Design and layout by Sara Radka
Edited by Nikki Ramsay
Copyedited by Renae Gilles and Kristin Russo

Image Credits

Getty Images: Apexphotos, 24, Caiaimage/Sam Edwards, 21, Cultura RF, 36, Darrin Klimek, 10, EyeEm, 27, Firmafotografen, 43 (bottom), fStop, 22, golero, 15, iStockphoto, 3, iStockphoto, 5, 8, 11, 14, 17, 18, 20, 32, 39, joe daniel price, 30; Pixabay: Newknown-4k, cover (vortex), Niedec, background (parchment), Raw pixel, background (concrete), StockSnap, cover (person); Shutterstock: Anabela88, 7, DONOT6_STUDIO, 12, Everett Historical, 42, Inked Pixels, 40, itechno, 43 (top), Kayihan Bolukbasi, 6, lassedesignen, 1, LittleDogKorat, 26, Oakview Studios, 28, Ponderful Pictures, 29, sergign, 35, Taras Verkhovynets, 38, Tyler Olson, 34, Vlue, cover (hand), zhgee, 16

ISBN: 978-1-62920-810-7 (library binding)
ISBN: 978-1-62920-818-3 (ePUB eBook)

full tilt PRESS

CONTENTS

NEAR-DEATH
EXPERIENCES

It is said that death is one of the only certain things in life. But what about when death isn't final? What about people who die and come back to life? Many people around the world have recorded experiences like these. But what really happens to those who die and live to tell about it?

Reunions with loved ones. Religious visions. A deep sleep. Floating outside of your body. These are just some of the things that people who have had a near-death experience (NDE) report.

Advances in technology and medicine mean that doctors can bring more and more people back from the edge of death. Sometimes, however, even the best doctors can't explain why people come back to life. What allows some people to stand at the edge of death and return to the land of the living? Are NDEs medical mysteries—or miracles?

A DAY AT
THE BEACH

About 20 percent of people who survive drowning accidents report having a near-death experience.

Ali Abdel-Rahim Mohammad had been enjoying a fun day at the beach with his friends. It was the summer of 1999 in Alexandria, Egypt. While swimming, he had suddenly collapsed and started to drown. Ali's friends pulled him out of the water and back onto the beach. They called for help, but it was too late. Doctors declared that Ali was dead, and his body was taken away. But somebody had made a grave mistake.

Just a few hours later, Ali awoke—very much alive, but terrified. The last thing he remembered was getting dizzy and seeing a vision of his mother's face. Then it felt like he was in a deep sleep. Ali's friends had called his family and told them that Ali had died from drowning. When Ali called them several hours later, they got the shock of their lives! Doctors didn't know why Ali suddenly regained **consciousness** after being declared dead. It was a mystery.

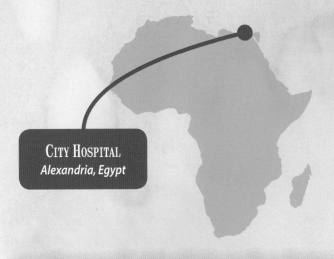

CITY HOSPITAL
Alexandria, Egypt

consciousness: the state of being awake and aware of your surroundings

The summer of 2018 was a deadly one in Alexandria, Egypt. More than 20 people drowned because of sudden whirlpools and large waves.

A COLD FRIGHT

Ali had never been so cold before. The last thing he remembered was the heat of the sun at the beach, and then he felt dizzy and saw a vision of his mother's face. But now, Ali shivered in the dark. He could barely see anything. He thought he must have been in a deep sleep. Something had awakened him suddenly. A loud metallic clang. Unknown voices whispering. But where was he?

Who Decides You're Dead?

Who decides that someone is dead? Most people are declared dead by a doctor. The doctor will check that either the heartbeat or breathing has stopped completely. In some cases, a person is declared dead when there is no more brain activity. A **coroner** may also make this declaration. A coroner is usually an elected official. Often they don't have a medical background. This may explain why some people wake up in **morgues** alive!

Ali's eyes adjusted more to the dark. He was surrounded by metal walls that seemed to be closing in on him. Ali had to get out! He opened his mouth, but he was too cold to make a sound. There was movement near his head. Slowly he stretched out his hand. Someone screamed.

coroner: a person whose job is to look into unusual deaths

morgue: a place where dead bodies are stored before burial or cremation

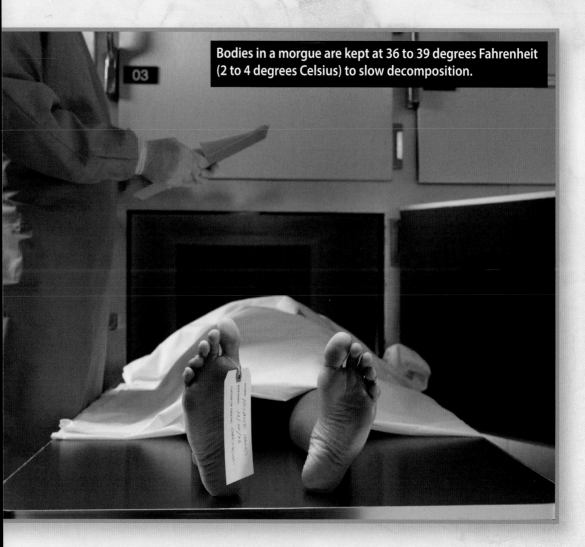

Bodies in a morgue are kept at 36 to 39 degrees Fahrenheit (2 to 4 degrees Celsius) to slow decomposition.

SHIVERING IN THE DARK

The morgue worker ran screaming out into the hallway. He had been about to close the door to one of the refrigerated compartments where the dead bodies were kept at the hospital morgue. All of a sudden, he was grabbed by the icy hand of a dead man. "Help us, help us!" the worker yelled. A family who had been in the morgue to identify a body started screaming too. They all fled the room in horror.

Ali was left alone in the metal box. He would have to escape on his own. Slowly, he dragged himself out of the metal container. He wasn't a ghost or a zombie. He was alive! And very cold. On freezing legs, he crossed the morgue. Ali wanted to find a phone. He went to call his family and tell them what had happened.

Many hospitals have a morgue. It is usually located in the basement.

ZOMBIE
GRANDMA

Li Xiufeng's experience earned her the nickname "Zombie Gran."

Li Xiufeng's neighbor, Chen Qingwang, entered Li's home. It was 2012, the day before Li's funeral, and Chen wanted to make sure that everything was ready.

Li had been 95 years old when she fell and hit her head. At first, she seemed to recover. But two weeks later, she died. Because of her age and the fall, no one was surprised.

Li's family lived far away. Chen had been checking on her every morning. He had been helping her with things around her house. Two weeks after Li fell, Chen found her unresponsive in her bed.

He pushed her and called her name, but there was no reaction. He checked to see if she was breathing, but couldn't feel any breath. Li still felt warm to the touch, which Chen thought was strange. But there were no other signs of life.

LIULOU VILLAGE
Guangxi Province, China

AN EMPTY CASKET

Li had lived alone, so Chen and his son helped arrange her funeral. Following Chinese **customs**, Li's body was kept in a casket in her home for several days. This allowed family and friends to say goodbye and **pay their respects** to the dead.

Now Chen walked into the living room where the casket had been set up. His mouth dropped open in complete shock. The heavy lid had been shifted aside, and the coffin was empty. Where was Li?!

Chen was terrified. He asked Li's other neighbors to help him search her house. They looked all over her property. When the neighbors finally found Li, they couldn't believe their eyes. She was in her kitchen, alive and cooking! She told them that she had slept for a long time, and when she woke up, she was very hungry.

Li's body was put in the coffin two days after her neighbor found her. She woke up inside four days later, the day before her funeral.

custom: a tradition or way of life for a particular group of people

pay respects: to visit someone in a polite way; to honor a person who has died, usually by attending their funeral

No one could believe Li had survived for six days in the coffin. However, people can survive for about three weeks without food.

LUCKY LI

Li was in the middle of cooking herself a large meal. After all, she told her neighbors, she had pushed and pushed on the lid of the casket to get it open. She had really worked up an appetite after being dead!

A local doctor said that Li must have suffered an "**artificial** death." No breath was detectable, but she must have still had a very weak pulse. Li was very lucky not to have been buried yet. In some countries and traditions, people are buried within a day or two of dying. Li would have been buried alive. It was also lucky that her neighbor had decided he didn't need to nail the coffin closed as it sat in Li's home.

In some parts of China, it is common to burn the belongings of the dead. This allows the dead to use these items after they have passed on.

Buried Alive!

More than a few people have been buried alive and lived to tell the tale! In 1937, a young man from France named Angelo Hays was buried alive after an accident. After recovering from his fright, he invented a "safety coffin." It contained a portable toilet and a radio transmitter. He hoped to save others from the same experience.

Li was less lucky in one way, though. In Chinese tradition, after someone dies, their belongings are burned. Li lost almost all of her possessions. But she was still lucky to be alive.

artificial: not real, natural, or true

ALIVE
AND KICKING

Body bags are used for moving dead bodies and sometimes during storage at a morgue. They are made of thick plastic to prevent bodily fluids from leaking.

The first time Walter Williams died, he was at his home in Mississippi in 2014. Walter was 78 years old and had been very sick with a heart problem. When he died, the nurse who had been taking care of him checked for a pulse. There was none. Then the coroner came to his home. He couldn't find a pulse either, so he declared Walter dead. Walter was placed in a body bag and moved to a funeral home. The funeral home director and coroner were starting to arrange the equipment to prepare Walter for burial. All of a sudden, there was movement from the bag! Walter's legs were kicking. He had started breathing again and had a weak pulse.

PORTER AND SONS
FUNERAL HOME
Lexington, Mississippi

A FAMILY MIRACLE

The funeral home director called an ambulance immediately. Walter was taken to the hospital. Walter's daughter Gracie couldn't believe it when she got the phone call in the middle of the night. Her father had been dead, and now they were telling her that it was all a mistake.

Several family members had even been with him when he died. One of his daughters was a nurse. She too had checked for a pulse and found nothing. Now Walter's large family—children, grandchildren, and great-grandchildren—were all heading to the hospital to see for themselves. They were confused, but also overjoyed.

The shock of a loved one's death can cause numbness, anxiety, and trouble sleeping.

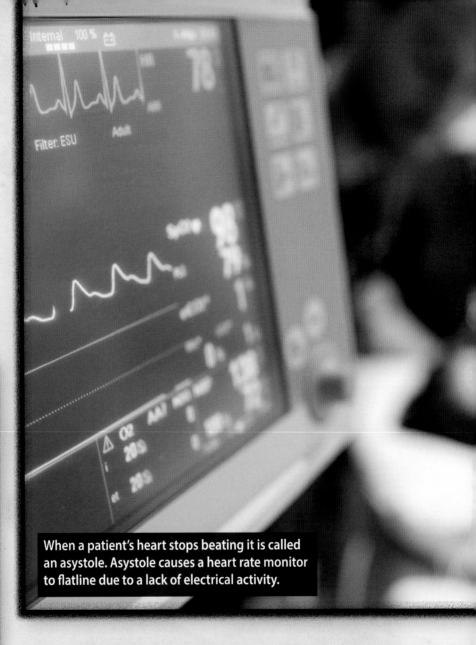

When a patient's heart stops beating it is called an asystole. Asystole causes a heart rate monitor to flatline due to a lack of electrical activity.

Walter told them he had just been sleeping, and then he woke up in the hospital. "No," his daughter Sarah said, "Daddy, you were dead." Walter was lively and alert in the hospital, especially considering he had been dead just hours before. His sister flew in from out of town to see him. And Walter got to meet his newest grandchild.

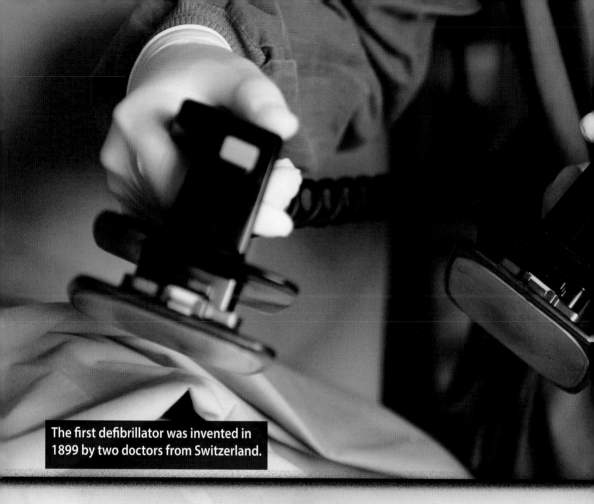

The first defibrillator was invented in 1899 by two doctors from Switzerland.

GONE AGAIN

Two weeks later, Walter died again. This time there was no mistake. There was no coming back. Walter's family handled the news surprisingly well. After all, they had been through it all before. They felt like the extra two weeks they got with their father and grandfather was a miracle.

Doctors now think there were several possible reasons Walter was wrongly declared dead. One possible explanation is that his blood sugar had dropped to very low levels. This can cause people to faint or black out. It might have caused a weak pulse that was difficult to find.

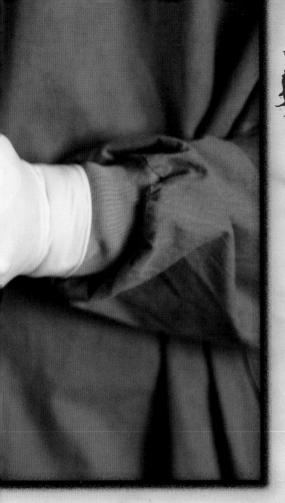

Dead or Alive...?

Certain medical conditions can make it appear that people are dead when they're really still alive. This may have been the case with Walter Williams and his low blood sugar levels. In a condition called catalepsy, the body goes rigid and does not react to stimuli. Breathing slows down and is almost undetectable. The same thing can happen to breathing and heart rates during a state of hypothermia. Hypothermia is when the body drops to dangerously low temperatures.

Another possibility is that he did die, but the **defibrillator** that had been implanted in his chest earlier brought him back. A defibrillator is a device that is placed under the skin. When it detects a problem with the heartbeat, it delivers an electric shock to make the heart start beating regularly again. Whatever the case, Walter's family was happy to have had a little extra time with him.

defibrillator: a device that sends an electric shock through the body to help fix an abnormal heartbeat

A WALK
WITH GOD

People have been driving and racing
dune buggies since the 1950s and 1960s.

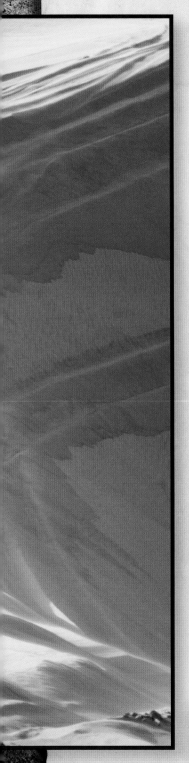

Trenton McKinley was 13 years old in 2018. His friend had invited him over to go for a ride on a **dune buggy**. The boys couldn't wait to try it out. They attached a wagon to the back, and off they went! But a few minutes into the ride, something went wrong. Trenton's friend suddenly hit the brakes on the dune buggy. The wagon in which Trenton had been sitting flipped over. Trenton was flung from the wagon. He hit his head on concrete. Then, to make things worse, the wagon landed on his head. That was the last thing Trenton remembered before everything went black. He was rushed to the hospital in an ambulance. Things didn't look good.

UNIVERSITY OF ALABAMA HOSPITAL
Birmingham, Alabama

dune buggy: a lightweight vehicle with large wheels that is used to drive on sand, usually for fun

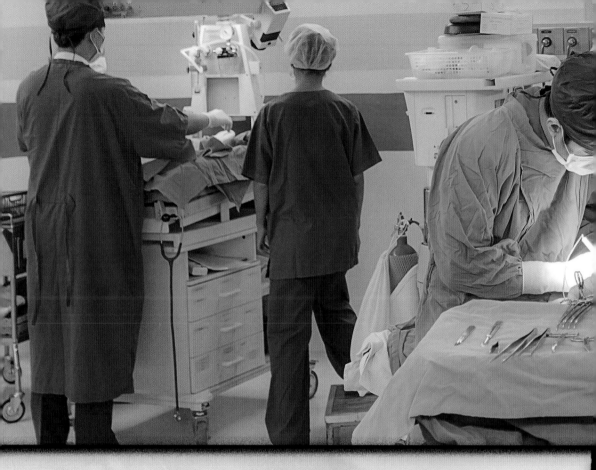

A DIFFICULT DECISION

At the hospital, Trenton was raced into the operating room for emergency surgery. He had seven fractures in his skull. His body was badly injured. Trenton's heart stopped while he was on the operating table. Doctors gave him a shot of **adrenaline**, which started his heart again. They had brought him back from the dead.

After that, Trenton died three more times—once for 15 minutes. Doctors brought him back each time. The last time, his brain showed no signs of activity. With the help of machines, his body was able to breathe. His heart was beating, but only because the doctors kept pumping adrenaline into it. He was **brain-dead**, and doctors said he would never regain consciousness.

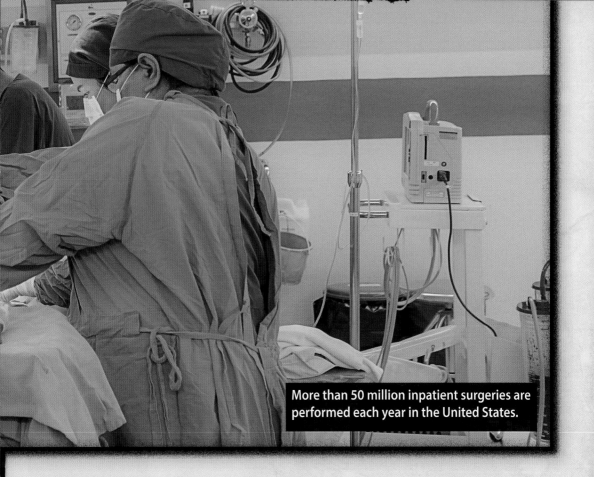

More than 50 million inpatient surgeries are performed each year in the United States.

Trenton's mom Jennifer made the decision to have his organs donated. It wouldn't bring her son back, but it would help kids who were sick to live longer. Something good would come out of Trenton's death.

adrenaline: a chemical that is released in the body when feeling strong fear, excitement, or energy

brain-dead: showing no activity in the brain

SEEING GOD

The paperwork was signed for the donation, and everything was in order. Then Trenton's hand moved. And then his foot. Doctors started to measure some brain activity. He was regaining consciousness! Trenton's mom knew it was a miracle.

Trenton's eyes fluttered open. His mom was shocked at what she saw. His eyes had completely changed color. Before they had been blue, but now they were green with white flecks. Jennifer knew he had been through something incredible.

Trenton told his mom and the doctors what he had seen while he was dead. He had walked across a large field. A tall man with a beard walked next to him. Trenton couldn't see the man, but he could see the man's shadow next to him. The man was carrying a baby while they walked. Trenton thinks it was a baby his mom had lost before Trenton was born. Trenton told his mom that he had seen God.

Unexplained Changes

After Trenton McKinley came back from the dead, his eyes had changed color. Many people report physical changes after near-death experiences. Often they feel much more sensitive to light and loud noises. Some people report that electronic devices sometimes malfunction in their presence. They think that their bodies now have an effect on **electromagnetic waves**. Others have said that lights flicker off and on in their presence, or light bulbs even explode.

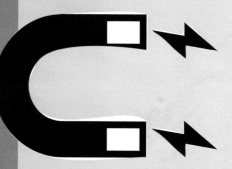

electromagnetic wave: a ripple of energy created by electricity and magnetism

Certain illnesses and injuries can cause eyes to change colors, although it is very rare for this to happen.

MARIA'S SHOE

In a 1990 study in Seattle, 23 out of 26 children who almost died reported having some kind of NDE.

Maria had a major heart attack in the spring of 1977. Her friends rushed her to the hospital. While there, Maria had a second heart attack. She died. The doctors had to quickly **resuscitate** her to bring her back from the dead.

Now Maria was resting and waiting for a **social worker** to visit her. Her name was Kimberly Clark. Since Maria was all alone at the hospital and had been through such an unsettling experience, Kimberly would check on her. Maria had an extraordinary story to tell Kimberly. While dead, Maria said she had an out-of-body experience.

HARBORVIEW HOSPITAL
Seattle, Washington

resuscitate: to bring someone who is dead or dying back to life, usually through medical work

social worker: a person whose job is to help those in need due to personal or financial problems

AN IMPOSSIBLE SIGHTING

Maria told Kimberly that when she died, she floated out of her body and up to the ceiling. She felt a pull to look outside and "**willed**" her body into floating outside. She looked around the emergency room entrance, and later she was able to describe it in great detail.

will: to try to make something happen by using thoughts and strong concentration

About 75 percent of people who have experienced an NDE describe leaving their physical bodies.

Maria soon felt another pull—there was something else to look at. She floated up and saw a shoe on a ledge outside one of the hospital's windows. Maria told Kimberly about the shoe. It was blue with a patch on it. It only had one shoelace, and the lace was pulled back and tucked slightly under the shoe.

Kimberly went to the window in Maria's room. She looked down to where the emergency room entrance was, but the entrance was blocked by a large shade and impossible to see. She looked at the ledge outside Maria's window. There was no shoe.

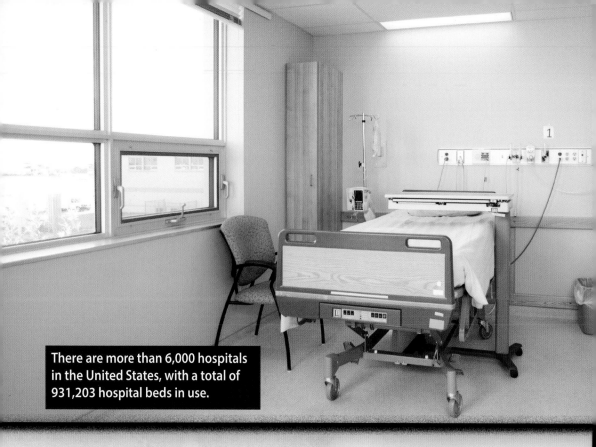

There are more than 6,000 hospitals in the United States, with a total of 931,203 hospital beds in use.

THE BLUE SHOE

Kimberly decided to investigate. First she went downstairs to check out the emergency room entrance that Maria had described. It wasn't visible from her hospital room, and Maria hadn't seen it when being brought into the hospital. Yet somehow Maria had described it perfectly.

Then Kimberly went on a shoe hunt. She checked out the rooms directly above Maria's in the hospital. She peered out the windows to see if anything was on the ledge. Finally she found it. A blue shoe, just as Maria had described. There was no explanation for how Maria knew it was there. It wasn't visible from her hospital room window. Kimberly decided Maria must have truly had an out-of-body experience while she was dead.

Out-of-Body Experiences

Having an out-of-body experience is commonly reported by people who have near-death experiences. Scientists wanted to study these experiences. In the AWARE study, scientists placed signs in certain rooms in hospitals where it was likely people who had heart problems would be resuscitated. They placed the signs high up on the ceiling, so that no one on the ground could see what was on them. Only people who had left their bodies and floated up to the ceiling would be able to see what was written there. So far, there have been no conclusive results, but the studies continue.

This knowledge affected Kimberly greatly. She lost touch with Maria. But she went on to **found** the Seattle chapter of the International Association for Near-Death Studies. Many years later, Kimberly had her own near-death experience and wrote a book about it.

found: to set up, create, or establish something, such as an organization

A TRIP
TO HEAVEN

About 70 people are killed
every year by tornadoes.

It was the morning of April 27, 2011. A tornado had just ripped through the small town of Arab, Alabama. And now, another one was coming. Ari Hallmark was playing at her grandparents' house just north of Arab. Her two young cousins Jayden and Julie were there too. Ari's parents drove over as soon as they heard about the tornado. The family grabbed pillows and blankets and prepared to wait out the storm in the house's bathroom together. They thought it would be the safest place, since it was in the middle of the house. The tornado hit. The strong winds battered the house. The bathroom door creaked and moaned. The house shook and tore apart. Then everything went black.

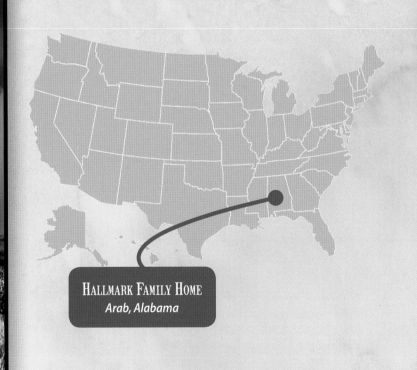

HALLMARK FAMILY HOME
Arab, Alabama

Many people who say they visited heaven during their NDE report seeing streets of gold.

CITY OF GOLD

Ari was knocked unconscious. She walked up a glowing staircase. Her father was there next to her. Only instead of being bald, the way Ari remembered him, now he had hair. His glasses had disappeared too. He didn't even have the marks on his nose where the glasses had pressed into his skin. Ari's grandparents were walking up the staircase, along with her parents and young cousins. An angel accompanied them. Ari thought it looked like the angel was both floating and walking at the same time. The angel took them up to heaven.

Ari saw big doors with diamond handles. More angels waited to open the doors for Ari's family. She saw roads of gold. As soon as they went in, their regular clothes were transformed into soft white clothes. After a little while, the angel turned to Ari and told her it was time to go back down.

Ari said her family was met at the top of the stairs by her grandfather, who had died when she was just a baby.

Most people report peaceful and happy feelings during their near-death experiences. About 20 percent of NDEs are reported to be frightening.

ARI'S BOOK

It took a long time to go back down the staircase. Ari woke up in a field. A man helped her get into an ambulance. Only Ari and her cousin Julie had survived the tornado. Ari fractured her skull and broke her collarbone and left arm. When Ari was well enough to leave the hospital, she started seeing a **therapist**. The doctor let Ari talk about her feelings and draw pictures.

therapist: someone whose job is to help people with mental, emotional, or physical issues

NDEs and Spirituality

Religious visions and visits to the **afterlife** are commonly reported in near-death experiences. Some people tell of seeing a bright light and feeling a strong sense of love and peace. However many people report seeing religious figures or symbols that reflect their own religious beliefs. They may see the god or gods of their religion or other spirits. Some people become more religious after a near-death experience.

afterlife: a life which some people believe exists after death

Ari told her therapist about what she had seen after the tornado. She described seeing heaven. She drew the staircase and the angel, who was tall with curly hair. The therapist recorded what Ari said. She helped Ari turn her story and drawings into a book, *To Heaven After the Storm*. Though the doctor could not fully explain what Ari had seen, she thought it would help Ari after losing her family. Ari hoped that her book would help other kids who had lost their family members. She hoped it would help them understand death a little more and to not be scared.

NEAR-DEATH FACTS

In **2012**, a 28-year-old waiter in Egypt had a heart attack and died. At his **FUNERAL**, a doctor discovered he was still warm and had a pulse. The doctor revived the man, and the funeral turned into a party!

A 1992 poll found that around **5 PERCENT** of Americans had had a **NEAR-DEATH** experience.

GEORGE WASHINGTON told his family that whenever he died, they should wait three days before **BURYING** him. He may have wanted them to make sure he was really dead!

Scientists have found **ANCIENT GREEK** graves containing skeletons held in place by **ROCKS** and **HEAVY OBJECTS**. Scientists think people were afraid of the bodies rising from the dead

One of the EARLIEST stories of an NDE comes from a book written about 2,400 YEARS AGO. A soldier named Er wakes up at his own funeral. He tells everyone of his visit to the afterlife.

The INTERNATIONAL ASSOCIATION FOR NEAR-DEATH STUDIES researches near-death experiences. It also provides help and resources for people who have gone through NDEs.

People often say that their NDEs felt more REAL to them than their REAL-LIFE EXPERIENCES.

Some people who have had NDES call themselves "EXPERIENCERS."

QUIZ

1 What percent of people who survive drowning accidents report NDEs?

2 Who declares that someone is dead?

3 Why was Li Xiufeng's body left in her home for several days?

4 What are two medical conditions that make it appear people are dead?

5 What part of Trenton McKinley's body changed color after his NDE?

6 Which organization did Kimberly Clark found after her experience with Maria's shoe?

7 Where did Ari Hallmark's family hide during the tornado?

8 What do people who have had NDEs call themselves?

ACTIVITY

Out-of-body experiences, religious visions, a tunnel of light . . . People who have had a near-death experience often report similar experiences.

Research more NDEs and write a list of common events that people have reported. What patterns do you see?

MATERIALS NEEDED

- Pencils and paper
- Library or internet access

STEPS

1 Use the stories in this book as a starting point for your research. What did the people in these stories see or do during their near-death experiences? Did some people have a similar experience?

2 Start a list of the different near-death experiences people had. Write down the type of experience. Below that, write the person's name. For example: *Out-of-body-experience: Maria.*

3 Have an adult help you search online for more stories of near-death experiences.

4 Add to your list. You can add more examples to the types of experiences found in this book and add more common experiences, as well.

5 What are some patterns that you see in these experiences? Could you group some of the experiences together? Into what types of groups?

6 Share what you learned about near-death experiences with your friends or classmates.

GLOSSARY

adrenaline: a chemical that is released in the body when feeling strong fear, excitement, or energy

afterlife: a life which some people believe exists after death

artificial: not real, natural, or true

brain-dead: showing no activity in the brain

consciousness: the state of being awake and aware of your surroundings

coroner: a person whose job is to look into unusual deaths

custom: a tradition or way of life for a particular group of people

defibrillator: a device that sends an electric shock through the body to help fix an abnormal heartbeat

dune buggy: a lightweight vehicle with large wheels that is used to drive on sand, usually for fun

electromagnetic wave: a ripple of energy created by electricity and magnetism

found: to set up, create, or establish something, such as an organization

investigate: to study an event or issue in order to determine the truth about it

morgue: a place where dead bodies are stored before burial or cremation

pay respects: to visit someone in a polite way; to honor a person who has died, usually by attending their funeral

resuscitate: to bring someone who is dead or dying back to life, usually through medical work

social worker: a person whose job is to help those in need due to personal or financial problems

therapist: someone whose job is to help people with mental, emotional, or physical issues

will: to try to make something happen by using thoughts and strong concentration

READ MORE

Lusted, Marcia Amidon, Ed. *Life after Death?: Inheritance, Burial Practices, and Family Heirlooms.* Global Viewpoints. New York: Greenhaven Publishing, 2019.

Rauf, Don. *Life after Death. Freaky Phenomena.* Broomall, Penn.: Mason Crest, 2018.

Stone, Adam. *Near-Death Experiences.* Minneapolis, Minn.: Bellwether Media, 2011.

INTERNET SITES

https://www.history.com/topics/folklore/history-of-zombies
Learn about the real-life history behind the idea of a zombie.

https://www.greekmythology.com/Myths/The_Myths/Myth_of_Er/myth_of_er.html
Read more about the Greek story of Er.

https://science.nasa.gov/ems/02_anatomy
NASA explains electromagnetic waves.

INDEX